ISBN: 978-0-9848818-9-5

Mary Ann Wolfzorn

Copyright 2017

published by

Woodcut Press

O'Fallon, MO

www.woodcutpress.net

Photo credits: Gene Wolfzorn

Additional photos: open source

Editing and book design : Neal Powers

A Return to Park Place

by

Mary Ann Wolfzorn

This book is for all the
Grandchildren and great
Grandchildren of the residents
Of Park Place.

This book is dedicated to my
Beloved Husband, Gene, who
Is my soul-mate for life,
And to
My life-long friend,
Sister Rose Stephen Cento, csj.

MAW

A Return to Park Place

by

Mary Ann Wolfzorn

The breeze made it a perfect day to fly. Two happy ducks were returning to Park Place to start their own families.

Sisters Bella and Della were side by side on this very special occasion.

It was a family tradition.
They were returning to the
spot where their lives began.

Even Grammy Duck couldn't remember when twin sisters ever did that.

They talked about the cool pond, the funny turtles, the trees, the birds, and the kind people who fed them and visited them every day.

They were almost there!

When they landed at Park Place they were happy nothing had changed.

Remembering how their mother broke her wing against the building, they landed very carefully.

Bella and Della searched for quiet places

to lay their eggs.

They needed shelter from the

hot sun and rainy days.

Mama Della's babies pecked their way out of the shells first. Soon she had twelve baby ducks. She gave them names that began with the letter D.

She named the girls Dotty, Daisy, Dolly, Dippy, Debbie, and Daffy. The boys were Donny, Danny, Dandy, Derby, Dusty and Dizzy.

Mama Bella's babies hatched the very next day, three boys and two girls.

She named her boys Bailey, Baxter, and Bentley, with Betsy and Becky for her girls.

The babies were cute and wobbly. Mama Bella and Mama Della were proud.

They were surprised their ducklings were walking and swimming the next day.

The courtyard was big. Mama Bella and Mama Della used different ends to keep their ducklings straight.

Since the ducklings looked alike, they might get mixed up. The mamas were happy when all the babies knew which family they belonged to. They didn't get mixed up at all.

People at Park Place loved to watch the baby ducks. Each day they gave them oats and other delicious things.

They laughed when they saw the ducklings learning to swim and climb up on the rocks.

All except Dusty. He was unable to fly out to land in the water like the others. He tried and tried but just couldn't do it.

One day he tried extra hard and his little wings carried him. The people saw how happy both Mommy ducks were. All the babies could fly down to the water for a swim.

Mama Bella and Mama Della loved the warm morning sun. It felt good on their wings.

Afternoons were wonderful for naps. Evenings were the best time to find things to eat.

The people at Park Place visited at all times of the day.

The little ducks were never afraid of people because they were so good to them.

The ducks loved the fountain in the middle of the pond. It sprayed them with water like a shower.

Mama Della loved to swim under the spray. She would flap her wings and get water inside her wings.

Her babies liked the little waterfall by the fountain because the water trickled gently on their wings.

Mama Bella and Mama Della stayed busy watching their babies. They did not have much time to talk.

Sometimes great big birds would swoop down very close to the baby ducks.

The baby ducks laughed when their Moms flapped their wings and quacked loudly to chase the big birds away.

One day the mama ducks finally found time to talk. Mama Bella told Mama Della about the first night she took her babies out to swim.

She said it was the scariest experience of her life. She tried to get all her babies out of the water after their swim.

Little Baxter just couldn't get out of the water. He tried but the rocks were too high for him.

He slipped and fell into a big black hole. Mama Bella didn't know what to do. She tried and tried to help him but since the big hole was under a rock she couldn't reach him.

He peeped and peeped for help.
Mama Bella knew he was scared to
be all alone in that very dark place.

Mama Bella quacked and quacked. There was no way to help. Soon a kind lady from Park Place helped Baxter get out of the hole.

Mama Bella was happy to see her baby escape. She quacked until Baxter got back into the water.

Then he swam around until he saw his mother. Mama Bella told Baxter she was glad to have him back with his brothers and sisters.

When the ducklings were nearly grown Mama Della called them together to announce a little day trip. She made them promise to stay together.

She was going to take them to a lovely lake near a mall where they could swim all after-noon. It was a chance to see how beautiful the world was outside the courtyard.

Off they went through the blue sky.
Soon they arrived at the lake.

They swam around the lovely lake all afternoon. They saw people walking, talking, and laughing. After a while Mama said it was time to go home.

Off they flew back to Park Place.

It didn't take long.

Mama Della counted her babies to make sure they were all safe and sound. She counted them once. Then she counted them again.

"Oh, no", she said. "Someone is missing."

She counted again and again. Soon she realized Dusty was missing. Everybody started to cry. "What can we do?" they asked.

Mama Della thought and thought. She told
them to stay right where they were.

She would go back to look for Dusty. Mama Della asked Mama Bella to watch over her ducks until she could find Dusty. Mama Bella agreed to watch them all.

Mama Della flew as fast as she could, back to the lake where they spent a wonderful afternoon. She couldn't find Dusty anywhere.

She quacked and quacked for him. What would she do if she couldn't find Dusty? What would she tell his brothers and sisters?

The sun began going down. Then, just before she gave up, the setting sun cast light under a bush. There was Dusty.

He was asleep. He looked peaceful. Mama Della breathed a big sigh of relief. Then she went to him and whispered his name. "Dusty? Dusty."

He woke to see his Mom looking at him. "Hi, Mom," he said.

"Dusty, I was worried about you," said Mama Duck. I thought I had lost you. I am so happy I found you."

"I am sorry, Mom. I grew tired and fell asleep in the shade."

She kissed him and said it was time to go home.

When they reached Park Place all the ducks flapped their wings and quacked loudly. They were happy to be back together again.

When the babies were all grown the time came for the ducks to leave Park Place.

Betsy and Becky called their cousins and brothers together for a family meeting that afternoon. Soon they would all go their separate ways.

Betsy and Becky wanted to share their favorite memories. The love they had received from the ducks and the people made Park Place special.

Betsy said they should take that love with them and
spread it wherever they went. All the ducks agreed.

"Just think! We will make the world a better place by sharing love wherever we go."

Becky said, "It's time to go now, everyone. Have a wonderful year. We will see all of you here at Park Place next year. Good bye."

And off they went into the blue sky!

The Residents of Park Place

www.ingramcontent.com/pod-product-compliance
Lightning Source LLC
Chambersburg PA
CBHW041634040426
42447CB00021B/3494